SEE / SAW

SEE / SAW

by Suzy Sureck

First Edition / Softcover
ISBN 979-8-218-32406-3
Published in New York by LumenDot in 2023

Designed by Suzy Sureck and Erika Knerr
Drawings and cover design by Suzy Sureck

*For Lisa who taught me to pull light through darkness with words,
and Dr. Modi who moves light through clouds with laser precision.*

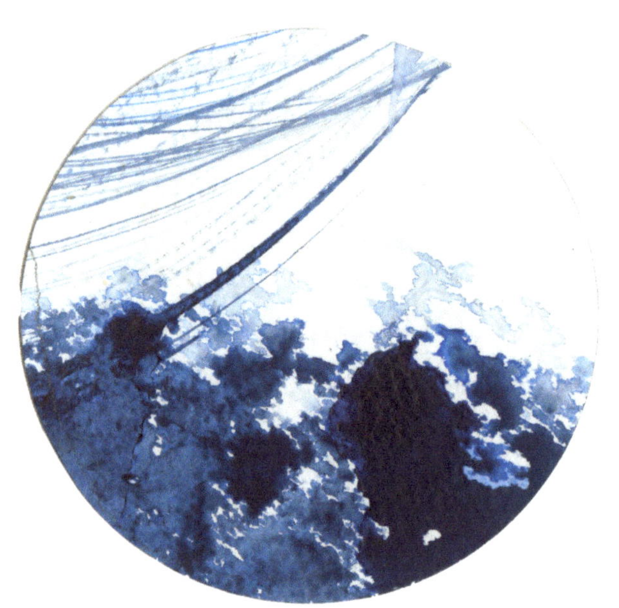

TABLE OF CONTENTS

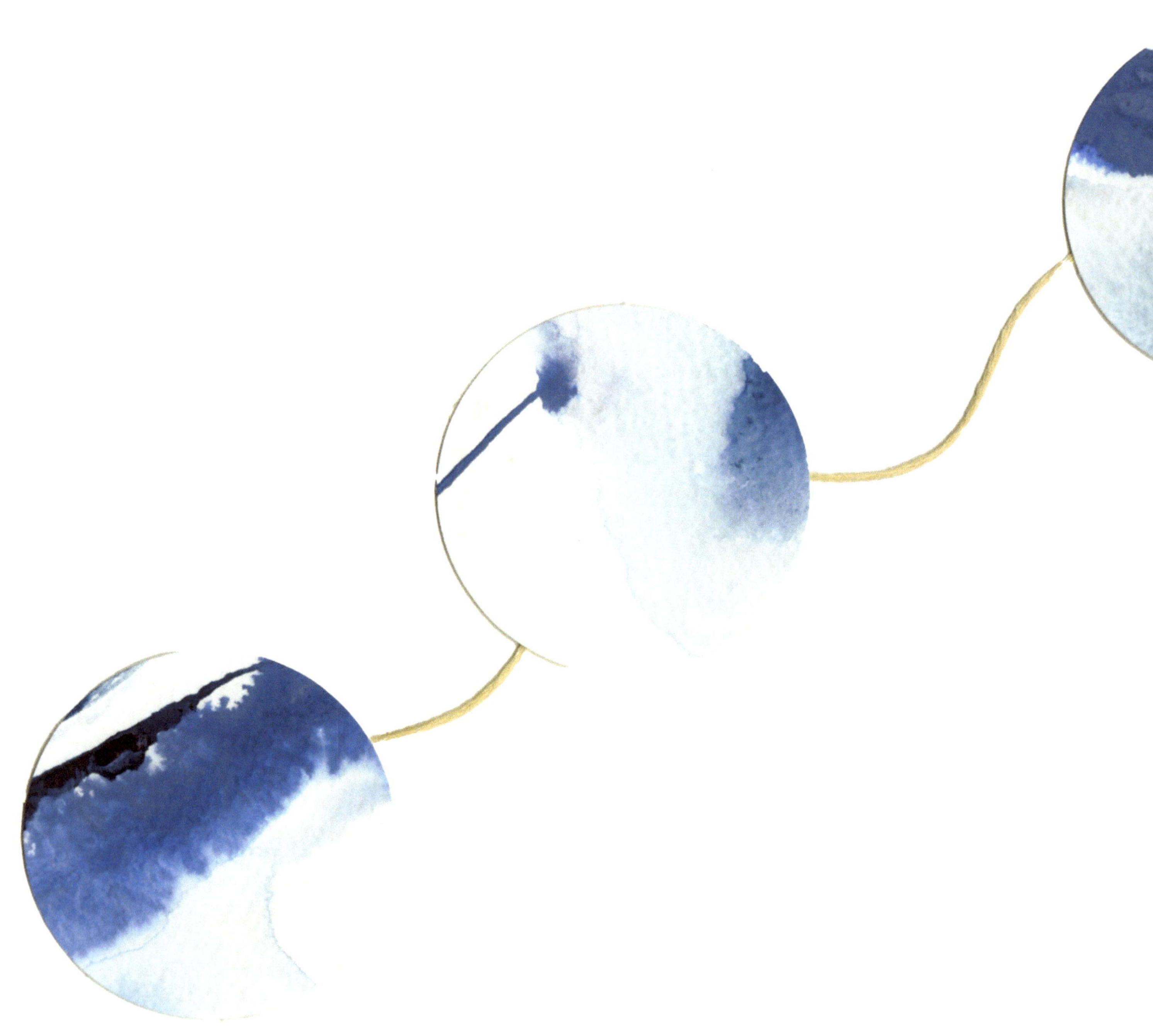

*The camera is having trouble focusing
a blurry spot where the universe is.*

Repairing the Hubble Telescope by Megann Snyder-Camp

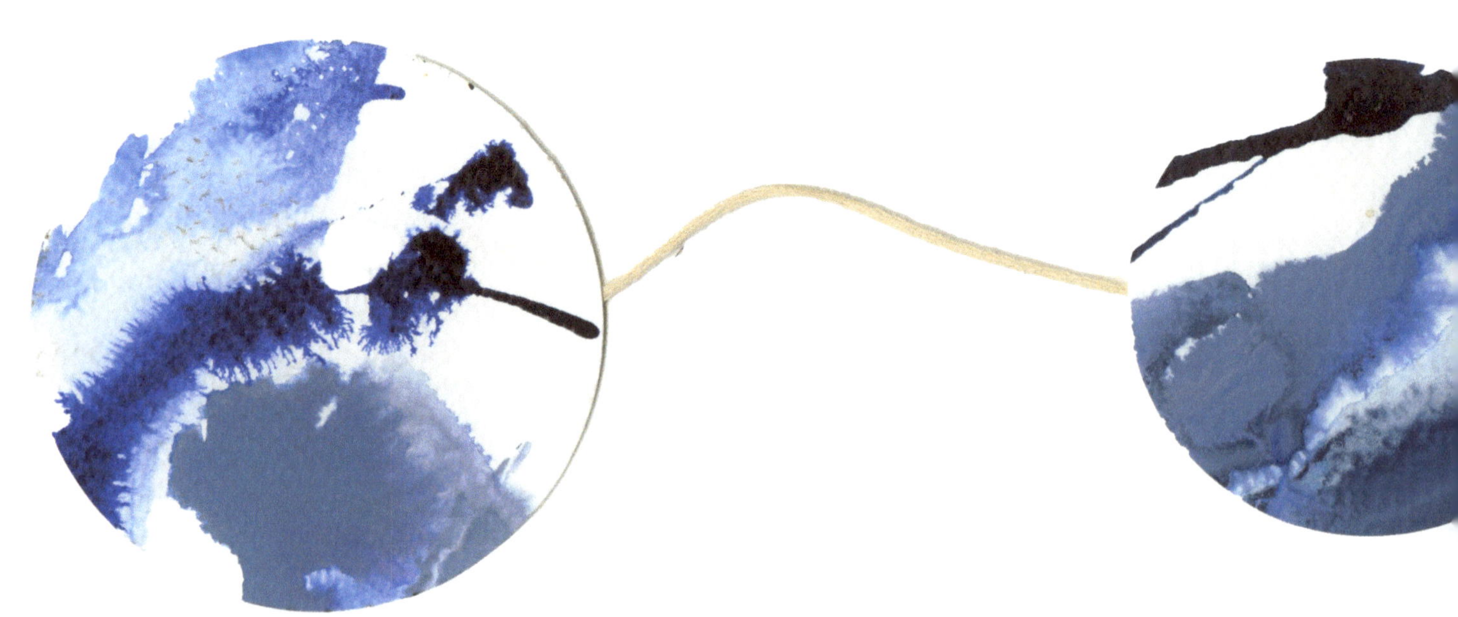

Preface

SEE / SAW is a collection of poems from 2021-2023, written on either side
of a procedure that altered my sight. Living with severe myopia, my vision with
its interplay of clarity and blur, shaped my perception and way of being in the
world. This changed in the winter of 2022.

The collection starts with a leap of decision making, translating thoughts to
words, and contemplating risks inherent in our human existence. The first part
of the book delves into my myopia as a child and its impact on my identity.
When my eyesight deteriorated to a focal range of 1" for my right eye, and
6" for the left, corrective lenses were no longer viable. Learning a change was
possible through surgical intervention triggered both elation and terror. Writings in the first section question the nature of visual clarity, along with a nostalgia for the blur, and a shift from the once familiar.

While sightings of hawks and owls are not rare in the Hudson Valley where I
live, the two birds of prey encountered while preparing for the procedure felt
auspicious, helping me envision clearer sight. At the collection's center, the
title poem SEE / SAW teeters between conflicting emotions. Encouraging
their coexistence allowed a pathway forward. The hawk reappears, and the
tone lightens with writings on drawing and cohabitating with the natural world.
The collection ends as a dream comes true, the ability to see unfettered in an
aquatic environment.

Ink drawings and prose poems weave spatially throughout, each circle offers
a small world of its own visually connecting the pages. SEE / SAW chronicles
a personal transformation and is an invitation for readers to reflect on their
vulnerabilities, perceptions, and dreams entwined in
the dance of clarity and blur.

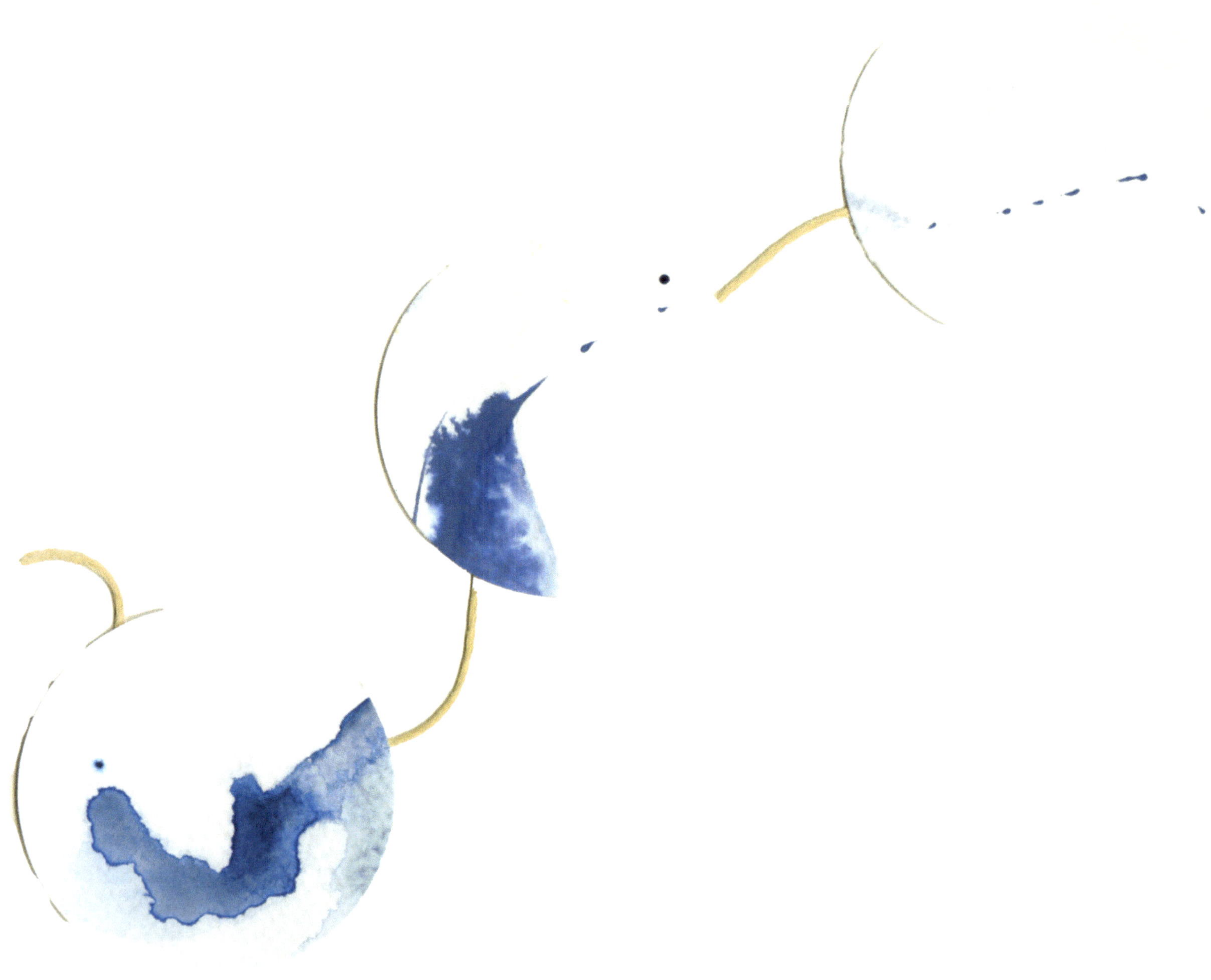

The Leap

Deep green moss envelopes her toes, pressing between each one. It surrounds the heel then ball of her foot, reaches high to graze her arch. Every damp, warm step springs her forward, heel, ball, toe, quickening until inevitably, the walk becomes a run.

Now feet touch down on branches that snap beneath the weight of her motion. Splinters and thorns jab the soles of feet opening her flesh. Blood dampens the forest floor seeping downward to rivers of stories. She no longer runs forward but backward along veins of memories where she hears the shriek of a siren from inside an ambulance. Perforated by needles and tubes, she is shaken off course.

Now her run forms a zig zag pattern. Here, as a small girl, she touches the texture of a crocheted pillow on her aunt's couch to know its form. There the girl holds a bat in the playground until a ball smacks her hard between the eyes before she saw it coming, splintering her pale blue glasses into fragments of shame.

She preferred the froth and salt taste of small waves at the beach. When they pulled her along, as tides do, she wandered back alone on the sand among smudges of bodies on rectangular towels, looking for her family by their brightly colored umbrella.

This erratic zig zag of her recall is watched by the barred owl who swoops down to catch her in his talons. As they rise upward, she slips each arm into the sleeves of his wings and together they fly from their dizzying fragments of memory.

Airborne, they breathe the night sky through lungs, skin, and feathers, dipping down to skim an inky pool shimmering in moonlight. Her feet graze its surface, breaking the moonbeams into thousands of light particles that close the wounds on her feet, gently healing the punctures, these portals of past.

As the sky awakens in shifts of orange and blue the owl swoops low over steep boulders made smooth by time, slides one wing then the other from her arms until the girl's feet touch down on ground. She is flying and running as she waves to the owl, her feet touching lightly on the cool stone. The motion is forward, so she follows. Forward, forward though she knows not where.

Stone formations jut outward until they can reach no more. As their form ends, she leaps.
She leaps until there is no sky and there is no ground.
Until there is only the leap.

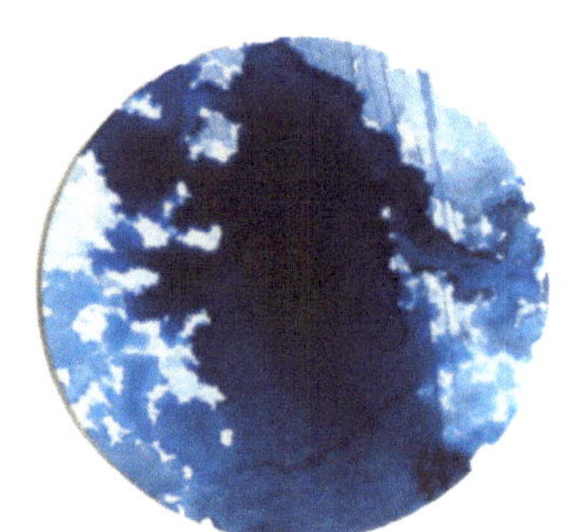

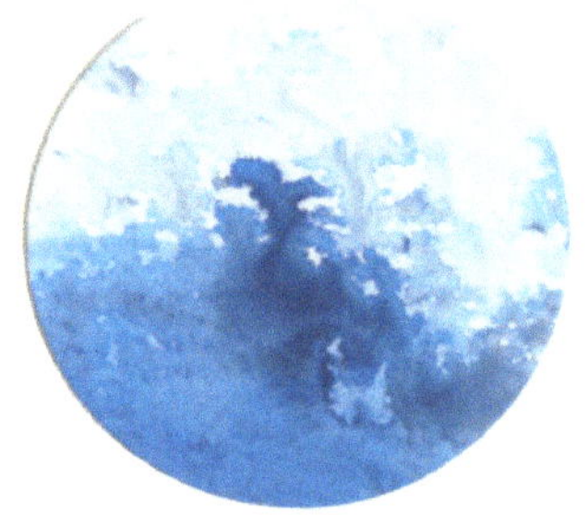

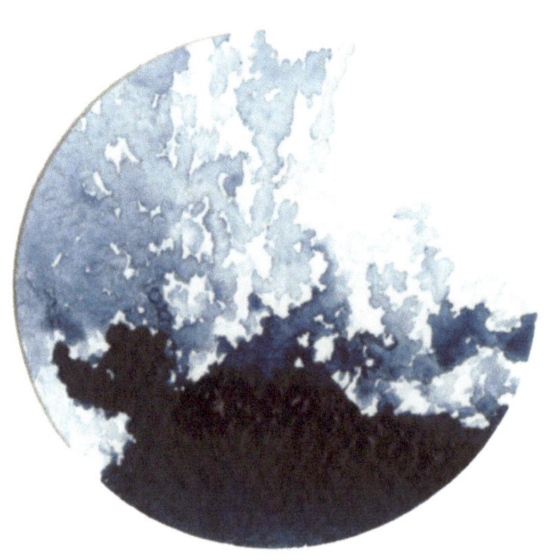

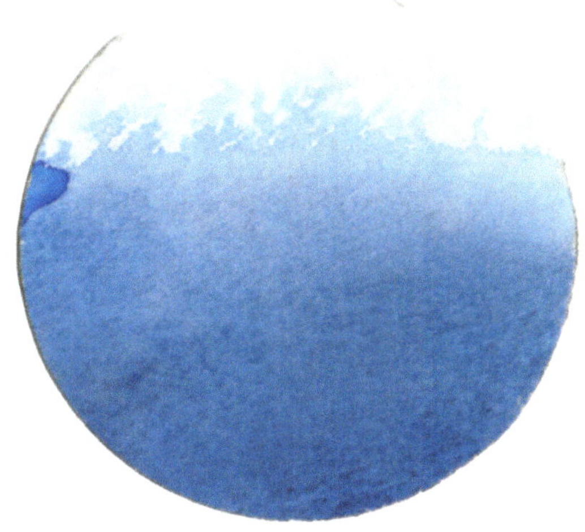

Nostalgia for the Blur

When distance was not mine to have
my eyes turned inward
to construct the brightness beyond my lids.
Outside a world of blur to me
and in this blur, I found my way
soft chair, soft couch, hard table edge.

Letters in hard books whose serifs danced.
My gaze followed their dips, pliés and elevés
at the small school desk.
Was I to know these lines could speak
a language others saw that I did not?

We are a team, blur and I.
Countless lenses, large and small, put in front and into them
bring shape and color to form with name
barely matching the vivid pattern of an inward gaze.
These eyes and I are locked in trust.

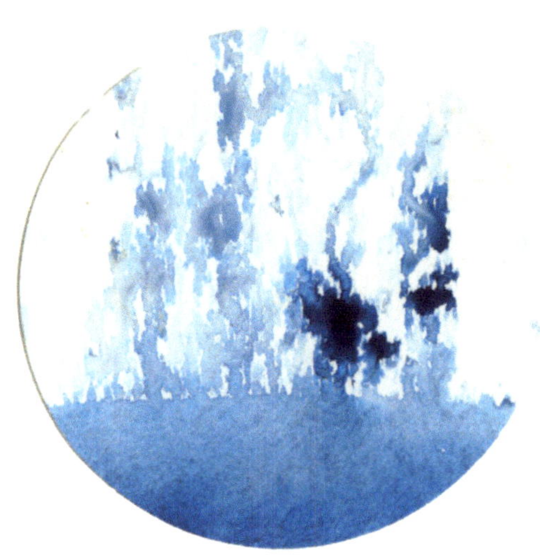

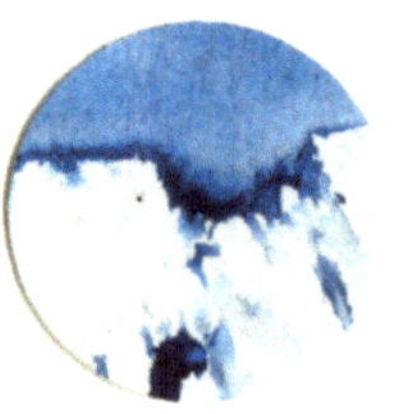

Looking Glass

Where's the border, barrier, barndoor
to shut between?

To pierce the orbs I've worn through life,
where is there to hide?

Without my bubble kingdom of thick glass walls
that bend light's edges,

how will I separate, delineate, appreciate
without glass shields between?

Balancing on light beams
within circling spheres

how will I bounce
when my insular bubble pops?

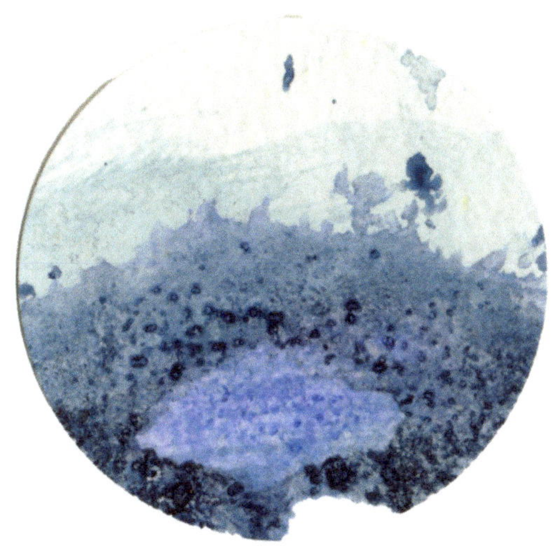

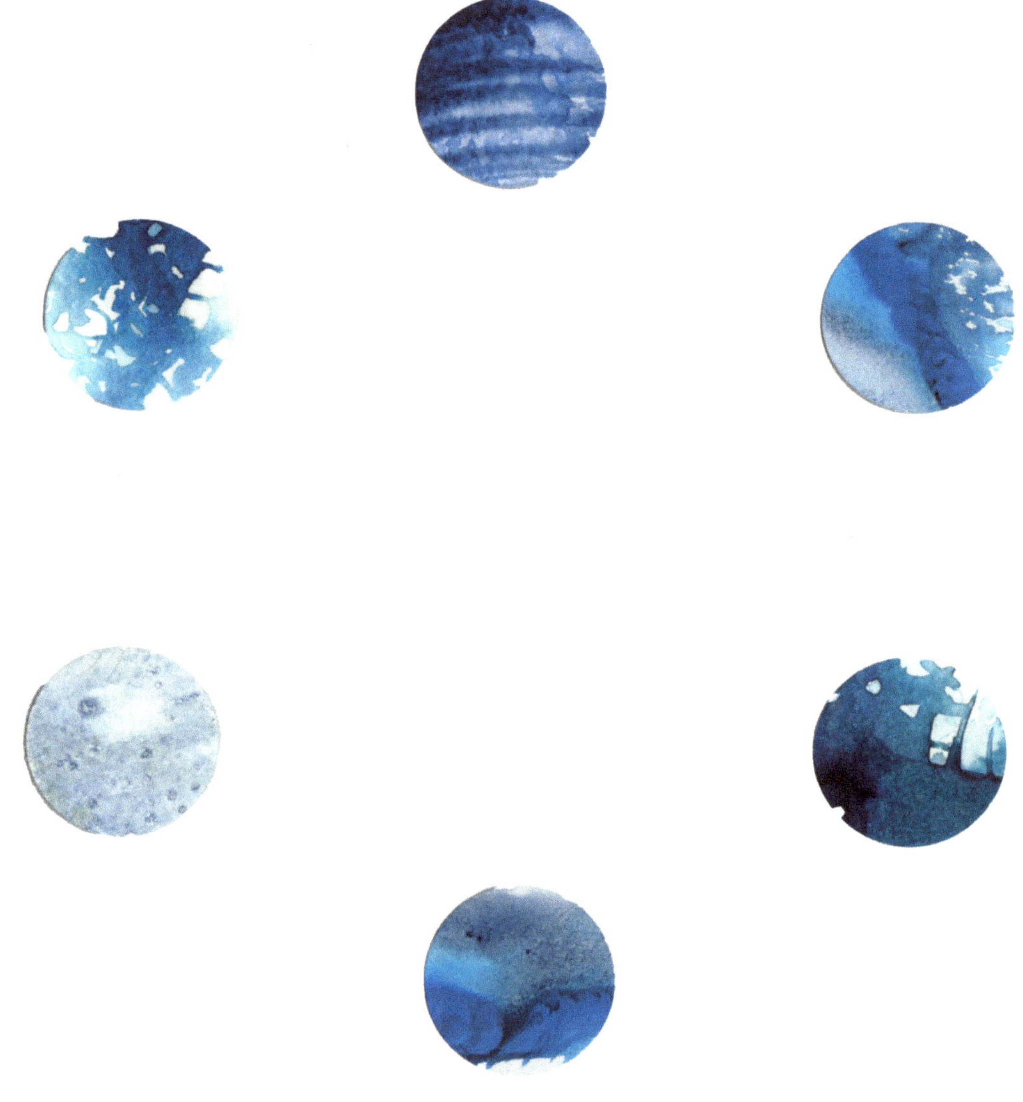

Jacks

We're on to something, courage whispers to doubt,
I'll keep you here in my shirt pocket,
the one by my rib cage
with the small red ball and 12 silver shapes.
Bounce once, collect 1
bounce twice, collect 2
until all the Jacks are scooped up
put back in this inside pocket
tucked in with the laughter of my sister and me.

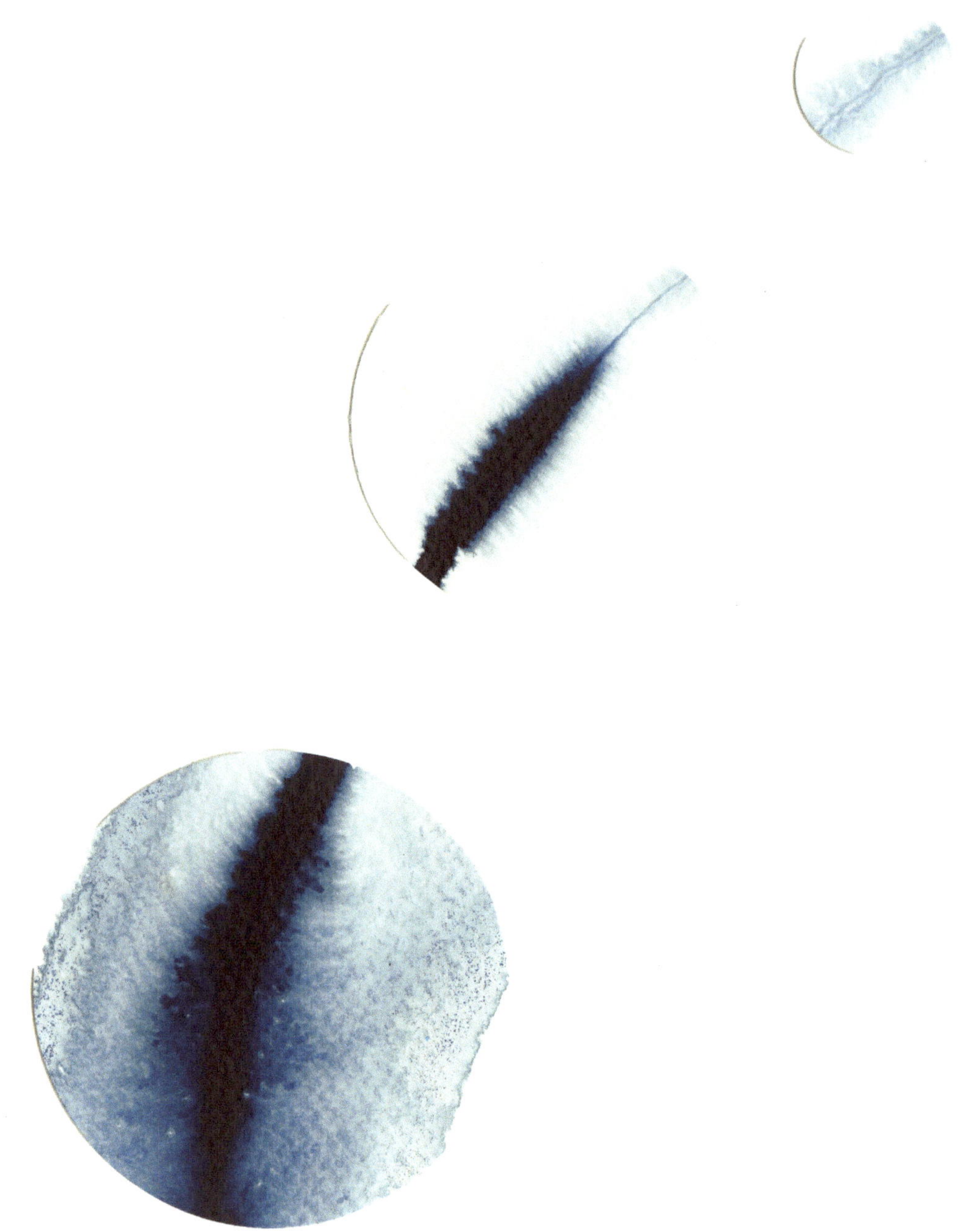

Blur Buzz of Normal

Embraced by blur, mornings have no edges
evenings return to dream

I rarely see stars others point out,
not red planet nor red tail of circling hawk.

Two sharp eyed birds visited last week
bulked in their winter feathers,

hawk stationary on fence post
waits in our locked gaze before taking to the air,

barred owl on branch glows in car headlights
her head turns, returns my stare open eyed.

Can I wear the hawk's eyes, the owls focus?
To overcome fear, I imagine

I am the hawk ascending from fence post
seeing the smallest details from circled flight above.

I am the owl, eyes wide unblinking
embracing exquisite details in the darkness.

Etymology

Feathers, like Faith, share their etymology in the word Flight.
An act of faith each time talons lift off, that the air
not visible, will hold their weight
each time wings extend, each time we reach or leap,
an act of faith to get behind the wheel at night,
when road signs have disappeared,
when signing medical forms that warn of blindness.

Slowly I place the feathered mask of owl over my own,
fitting it to my shoulders
turning my head at the neck, this way and that
to peer through wide yellow eyes,
taloned claws on knobby branch
precarious, together we leap

to plunge feathered headfirst into a bath,
scented bubbles barely cushion our fall.
Submerged, my eyes at water's warm skin,
body cloudlike below crisp soap bubbles.
This owl's mask has slipped off
I am again in the familiar blur of mine.

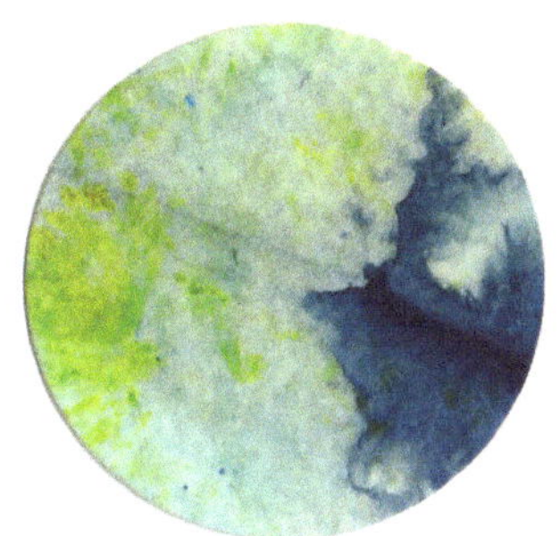
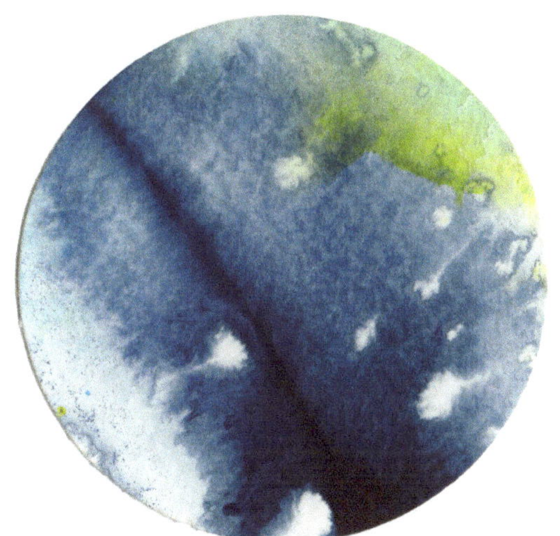
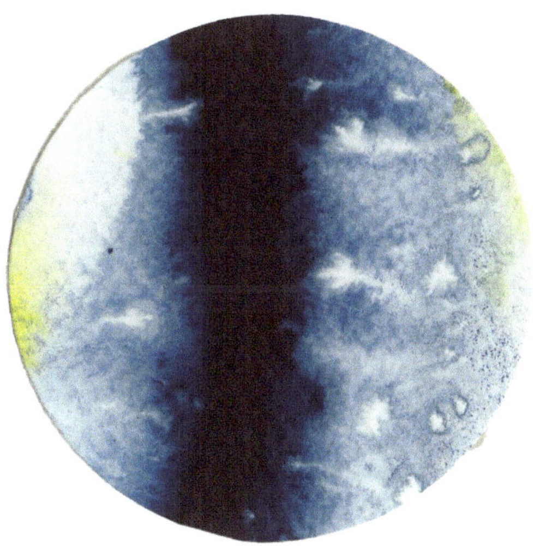

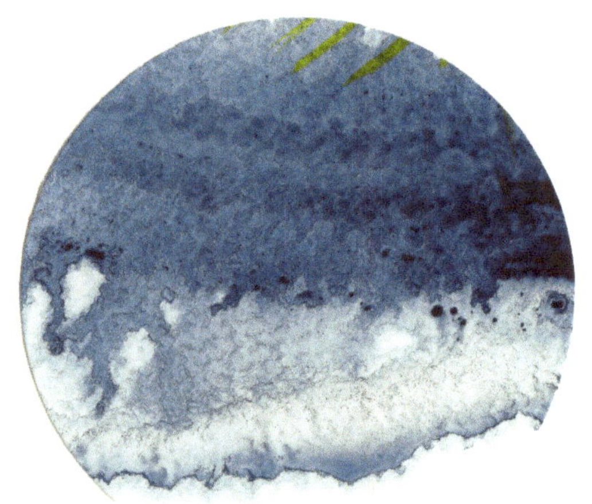

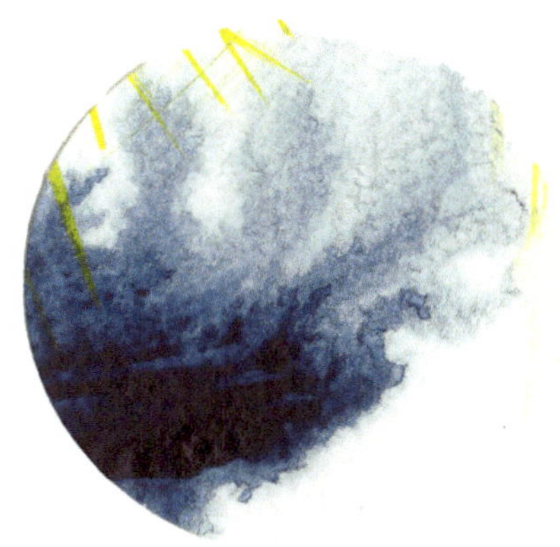

Repair man

Flashing topographies, riverbeds
branch from my optical nerve in fuchsia ribbons
past shrouded films perceived
at differing intervals by each eye
misguided, off register, off the charts.

Surrendering again to voyeurs, drops, lights,
I have come to the right repair man,
a kind gentle one who dabs my lower lids.
He offers lenses to replace
those in eyes that looked out
through blue cat-eye frames
with tiny rhinestones in the corners.
I picked them out when I was 4.

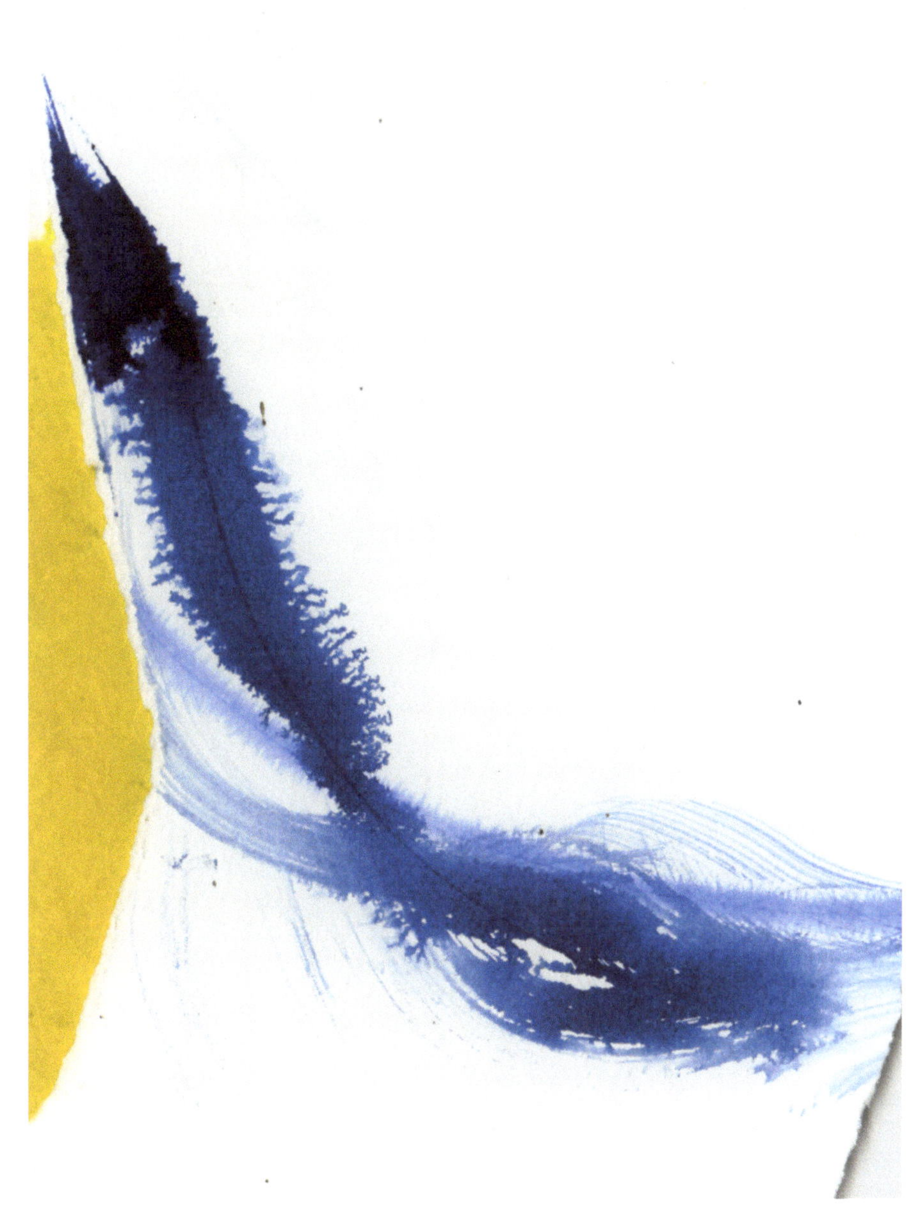

Swell Season

Woodpecker knocks at edge of my house seeking larvae unborn.
What lies in wait?
What sparks within the hollow?

To rinse the years of their past,
rid my house of old accumulations,
make room for a new decade.

This home a vault, a hollow to swallow,
to distill, disturb and comfort
as I bumble along its craggy path.

What has heaped up, swollen the cabinets and closets?
What can be born from its shadows,
when things are discarded,
and the dust is swept?

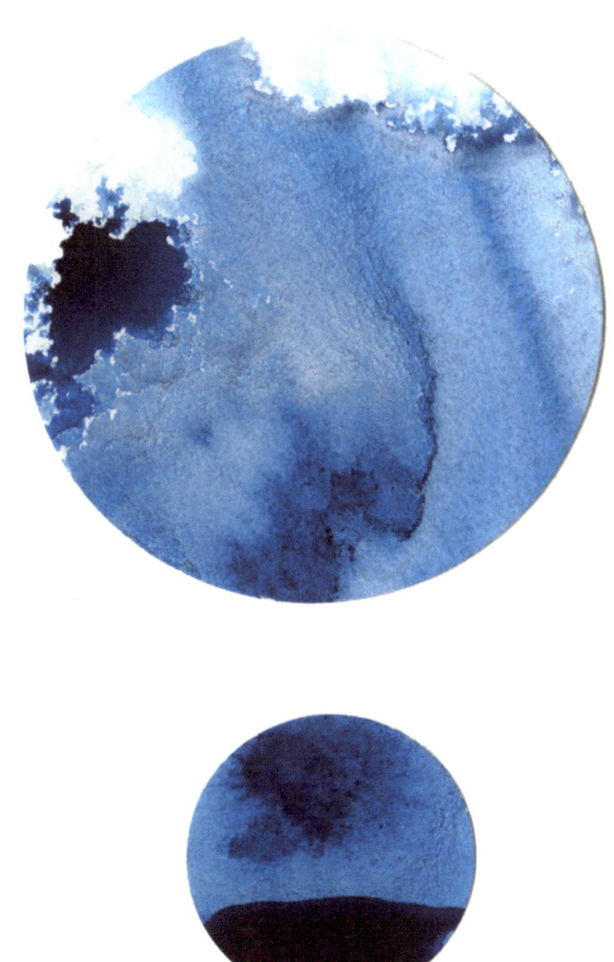

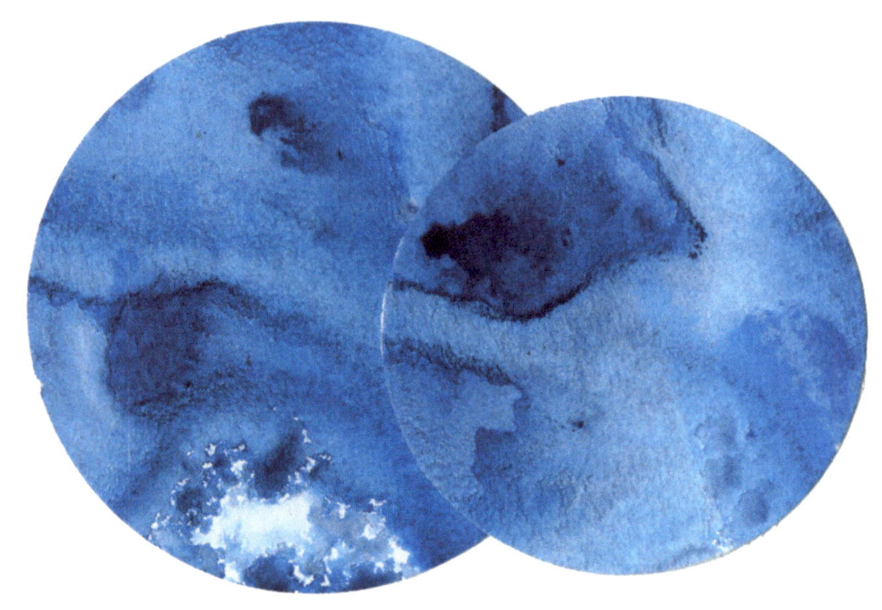

Approaching Radiance

approaching radiant sky
There are clear stars above, so they tell me.
When a bright full moon first
filled the eye piece of my telescope
its craters and all, sent me flying
backwards in disbelief and awe.

approaching radiant waters
As a child snorkeling with my mother in Mexico,
following her fins as she pointed to colorful shapes of blur,
smudges in the sea.

approaching radiant earth
Hope is ready, shovel in hand
though I've waited too long, again
to plant the bulbs
beneath deep snow.

What will thaw,
what will melt
in this approaching radiant world?

Clarity Can't Wait

Webb telescope images fill my news feeds
even shadows have lost their blur
eons of sharpened space
hurl forward through technicolor darkness
our eyes pinned open as the universe unravels pixel by pixel.

Deep blue shawl of night while
lens shatters in sparks across the sky,
negating blur. Clarity can't wait,
are we ready?

Familiar cloak of sky once
wrapped its gloam blue
suede of blur cocoon to
keep out the overwhelm,
will we miss the blur?

Galaxies come pouring in.
Faces, mountains, storefronts
streetlights are clear again.
We shrink in scale as
clarity fills a void,
dwarfing previous open space of not knowing.
As a universe blazes into focus, are we less alone?

Webb sends more images,
purple plasticine Jupiter swirls of finger paint
soon I will be able to see the tree's bark
and pages of the book it has made
but not the fine hair on the cat's ears, or texture of silk,
reserved for my gemstone cutters myopic vision
preserved in memory,
in this mind's eye.

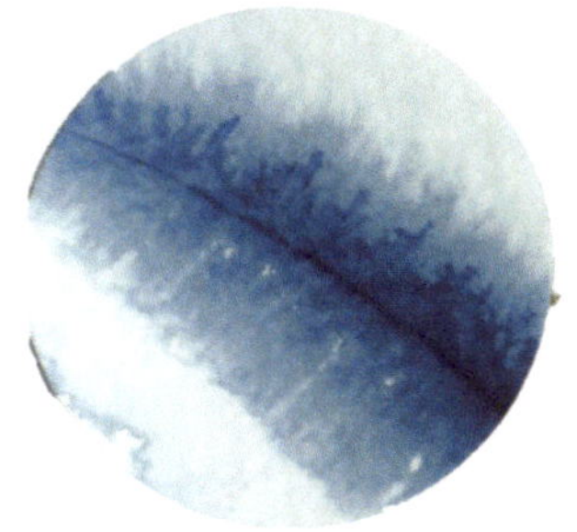
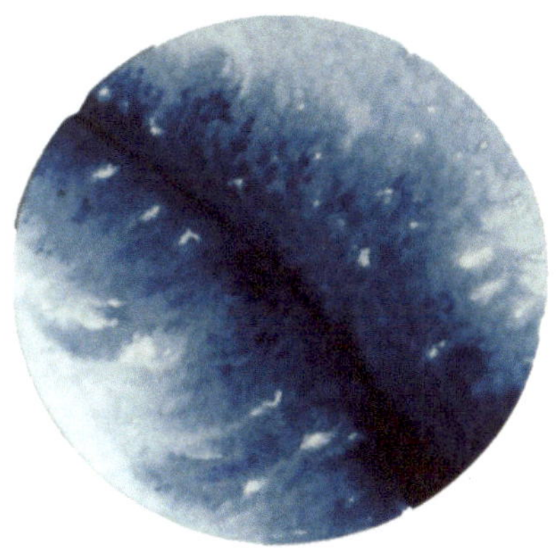
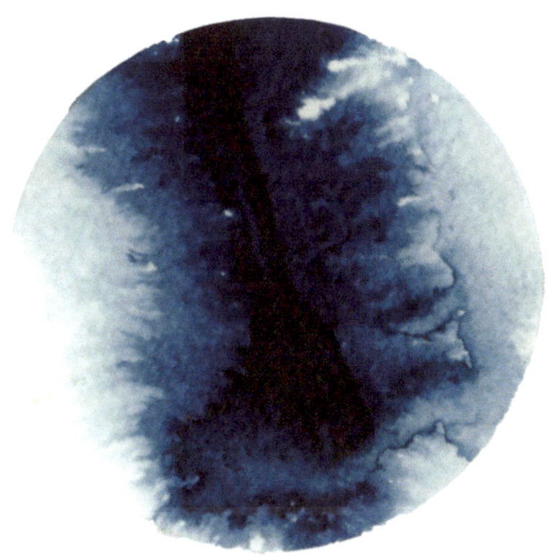

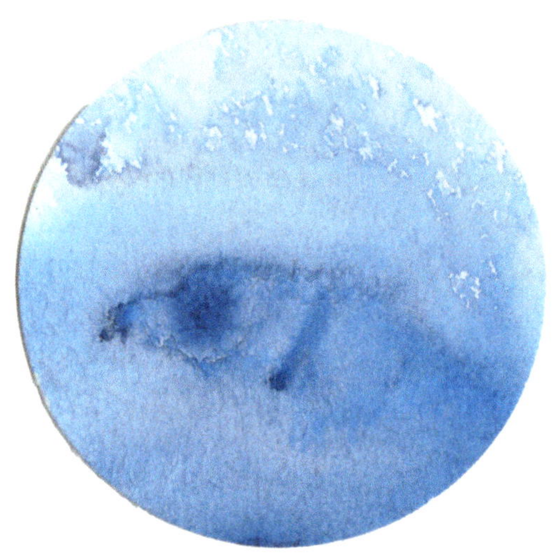

Possibilities

The hawk's mask
fits over deep indents
that bridge my nose.
from years of thick glasses.

Soaked feathers drip their colors
to pools of doubt
as we fold and unfold our wings
from today's damp rain that
clog our throats and beaks
seep through eyelids
closed to possibilities.

The branch we clench in our teeth and talons
could snap with the taught tension of our fears
or spring us
airborne to flight.

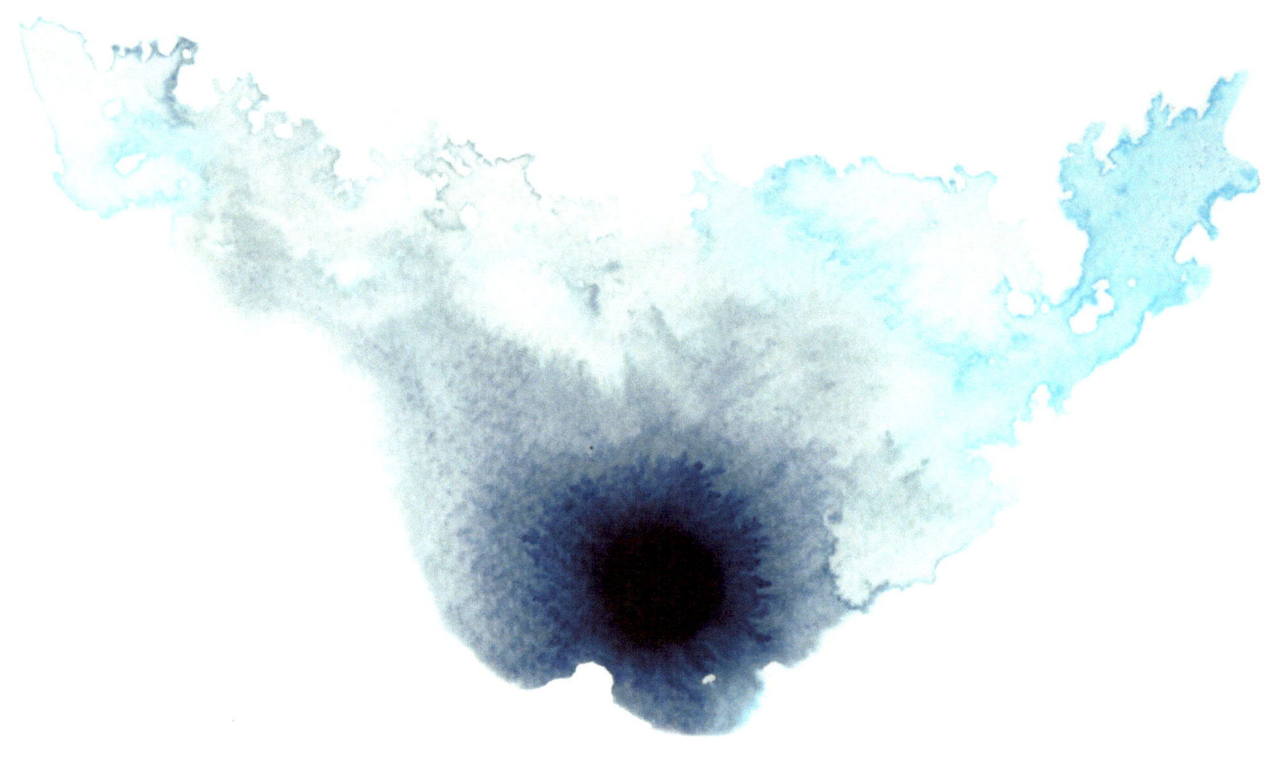

See Saw

Between patterns of rain on glass
a small yellow seesaw rises
in orange scented steam.

Two young girls
dressed in rain slickers and rubber boots
laugh as they bounce
backsides rise, bump down
the wood board between
lands in puddles of hope
orange and pink.

Up again to spring back
into puddles of fear
oiled ochre and rust brown,
see and saw
back and forth
until hope and fear splash together
mixing colors in their boots.

Peeking out from rain hoods,
Shana and I on roof playground of PS 59
on 57th street during recess
get up from our game
clasp hands to
stomp through puddles
of hope and fear together
laughing.

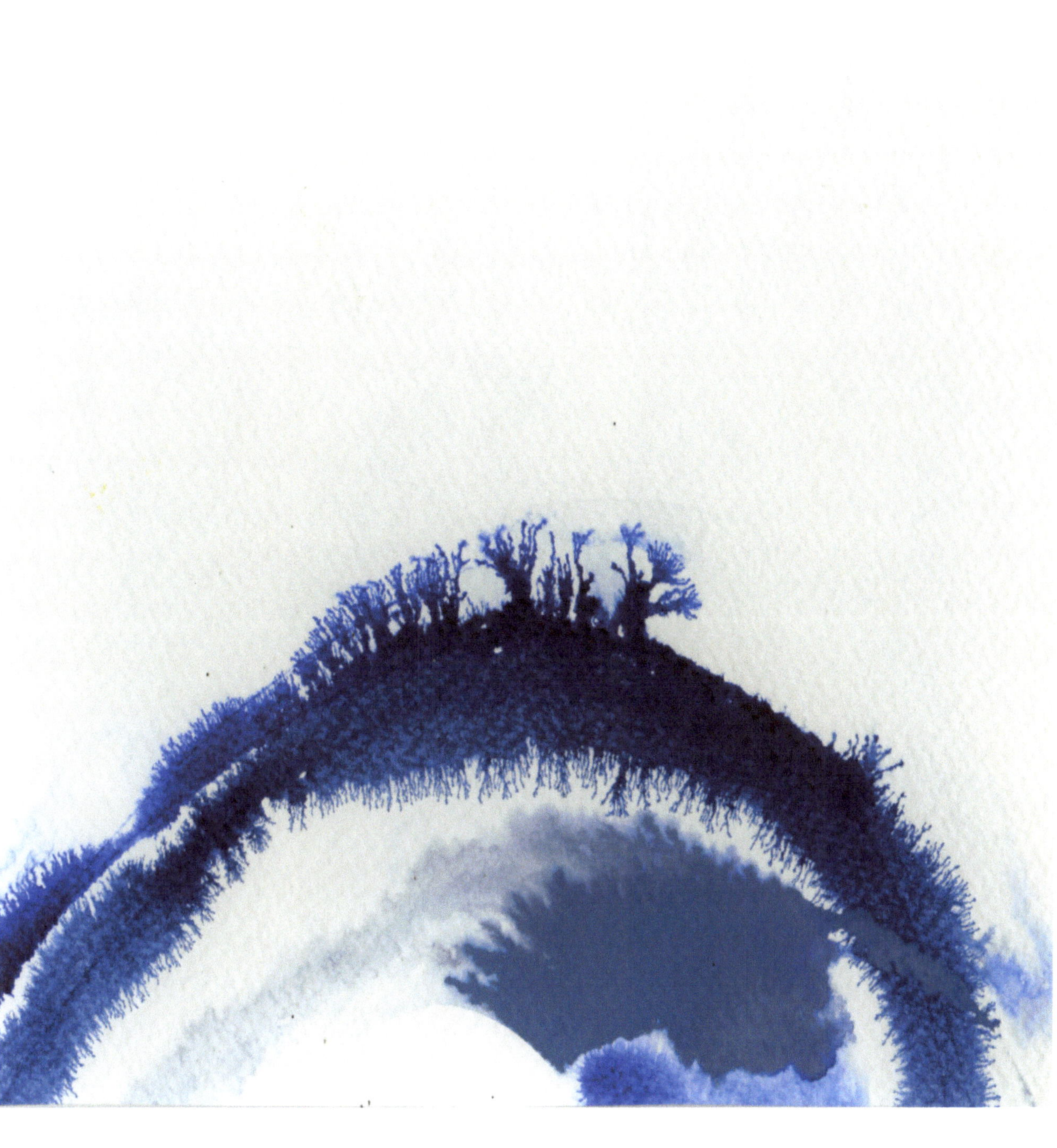

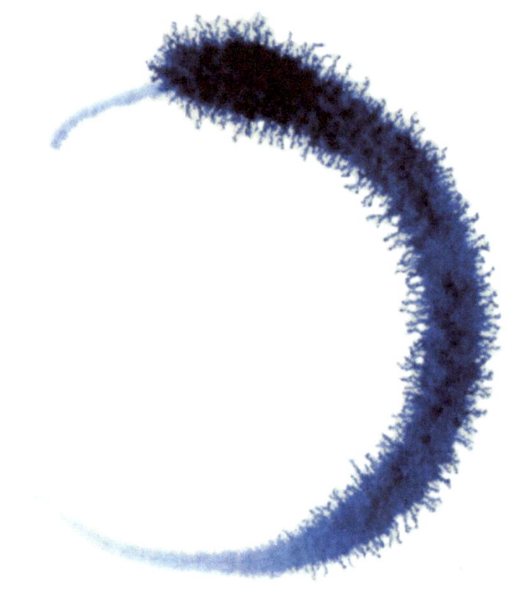

Enso

Serpent has tail in mouth
or mouth in tail
either way you look at it
we're spinning yarns and wheels

vortex gyrates
on wobbly axis
grab hold
this serpent life raft

drawing breath, drawn in sand
exhaled, exhumed,
washed back to the sea

sand piper draws,
the moon erases
its tale.

Fish tales

As she fills the cavity of her chest with a deep breath, her heart breaches its ribcage, reaching beyond the skin's surface. Bubbles of air seep out like sweat, drip along her arms.

She inhales a scent that swirls a deep lake within.
What do fish whisper as they swim along the canals of her ear?

'We fill you' they chant in hushed watery tones, 'you were born a fish before your grandparents landed on soil.'

 A fish with a tail drew as you moved, claiming its path in the sandy soil. This wandering map of your whereabouts drawing your steps, to be erased again with the tide.

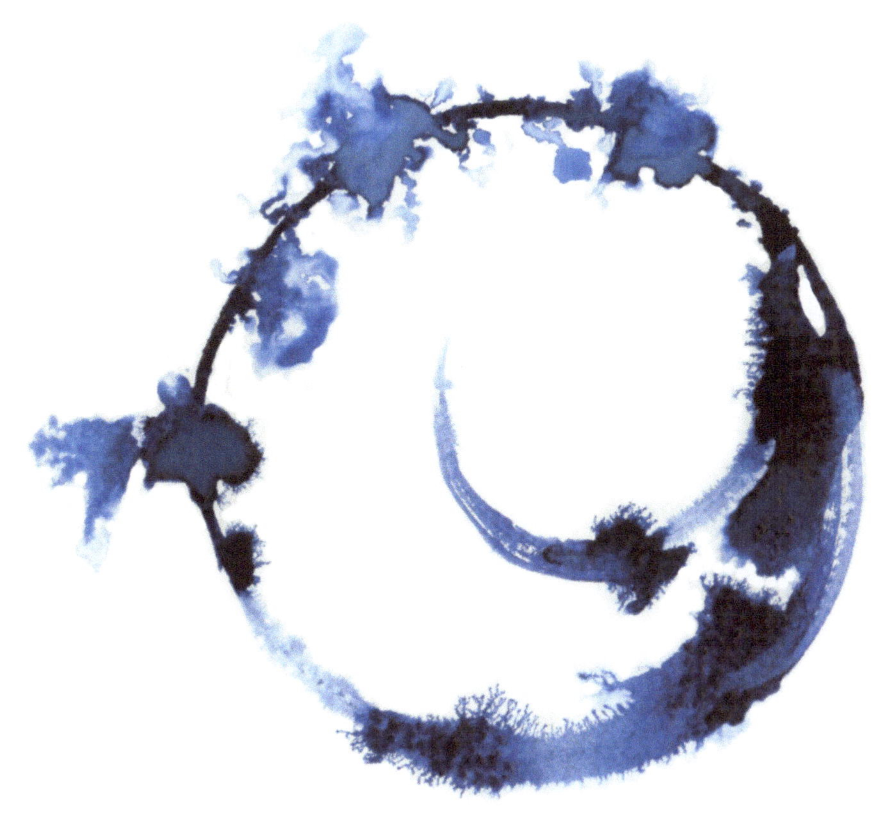

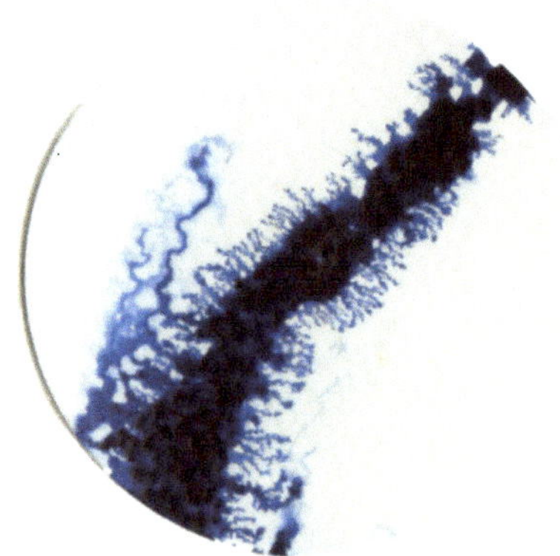
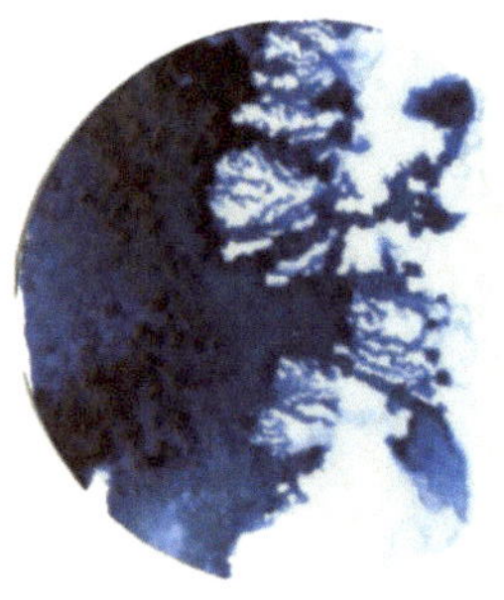

Good morning!

Darkness recedes from the glow of day
leaving a residue of dream

shy veiled imagery whispers evasively
as I crawl backwards into the night to gather more

slippery gems of dark
brazenly unravel into cracks of the morning

do I open my eyes?

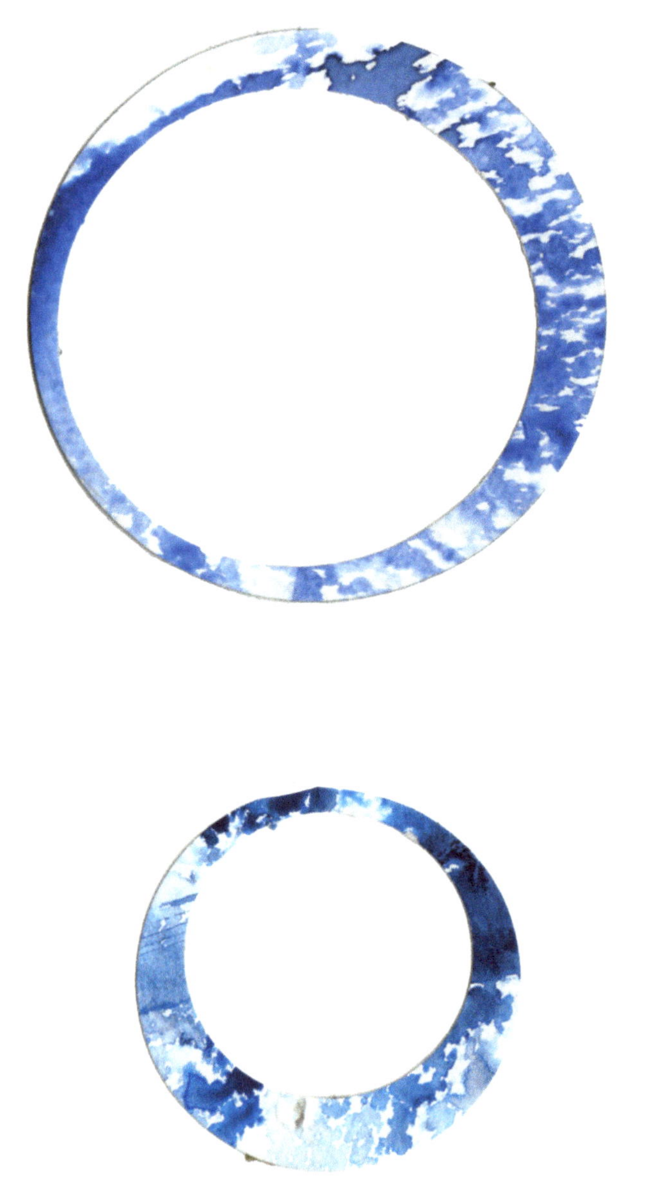

An Inside Out Day

She's turned herself inside out
the way the sweater peels off
reversed, crumpled
on the bathroom floor

not able to pick itself up
fold neatly
stacked up with the others.

It's not as bad as it sounds
the inside of things,
the parts close to the warmth of her body
the knitted yarns
of her mind
are louder than the weather.

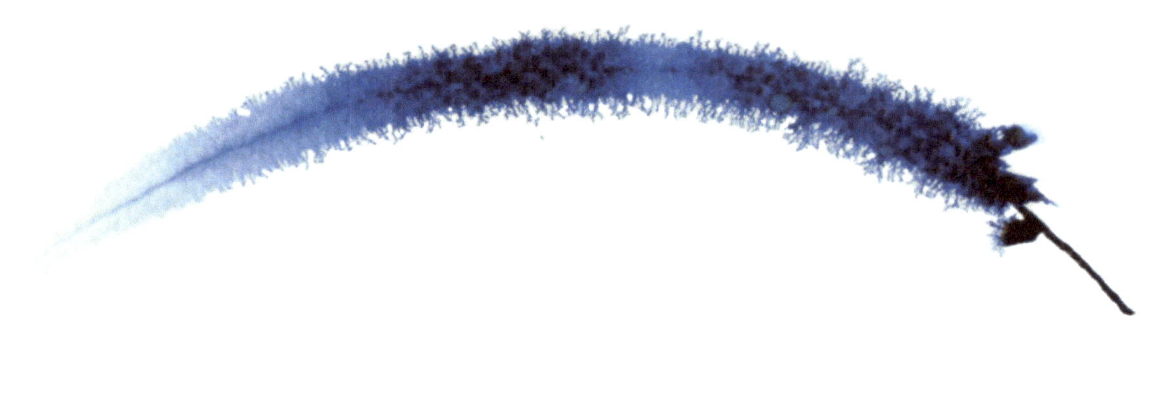

Messengers

Hawk and owl
offered their insights into sight,
let me slip on their wings
to fancy myself in flight,
seeing through distance flawlessly.

What got scooped out under bright lights,
as lasers calculated my new vision?
Loose dust from the past
floats in these elongated orbs
casting ghost shadows on new fallen snow.

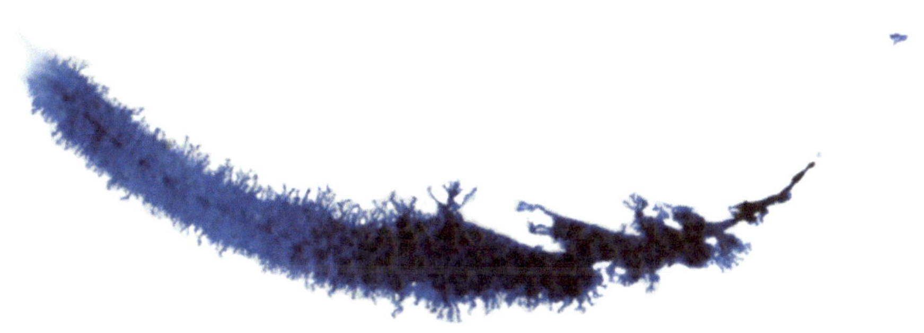

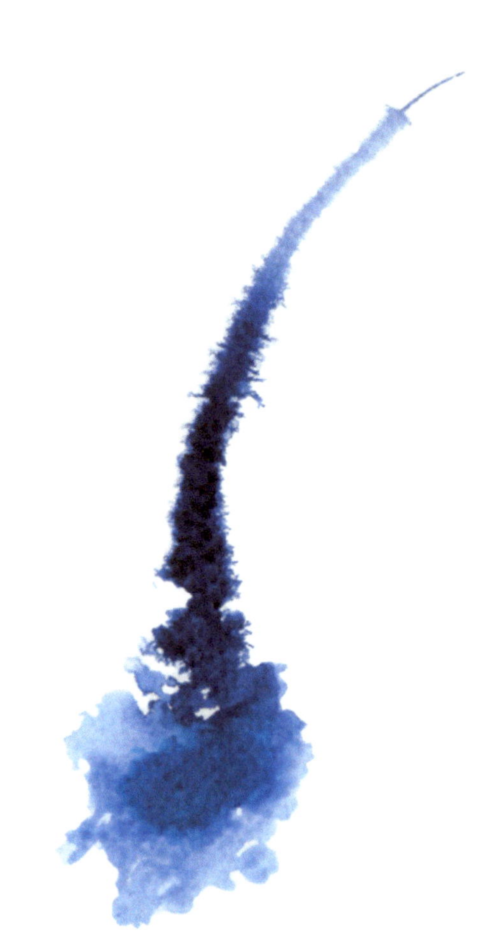

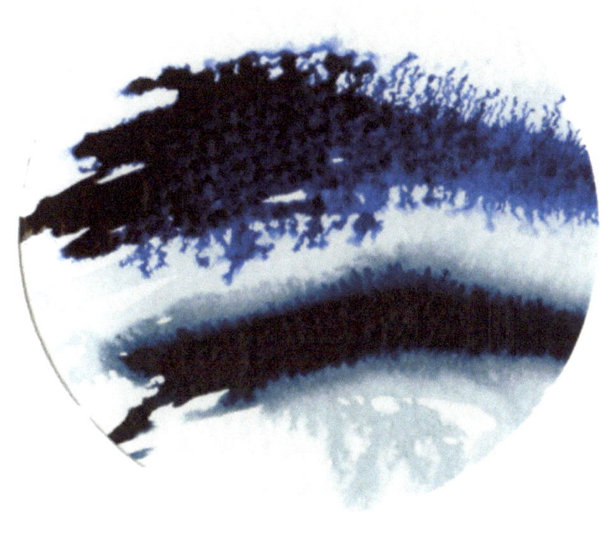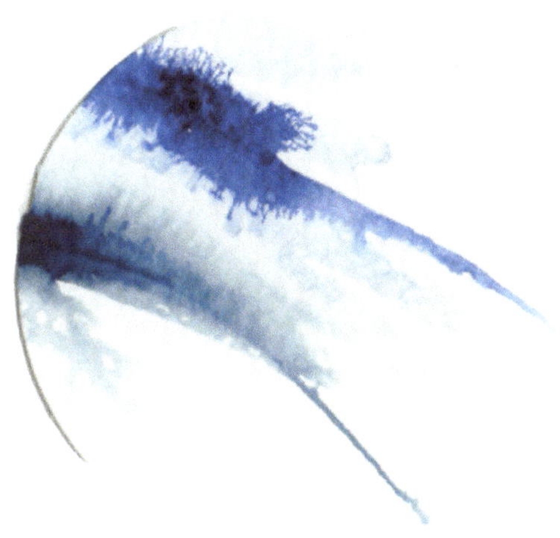

Pocket Book.

Write me into your pocket
your sleeve, your heart

write me into your full moon
your wind, your sailing vessel

write me into your palm's patterns
enveloped in these creased messengers

your palm
my palm.

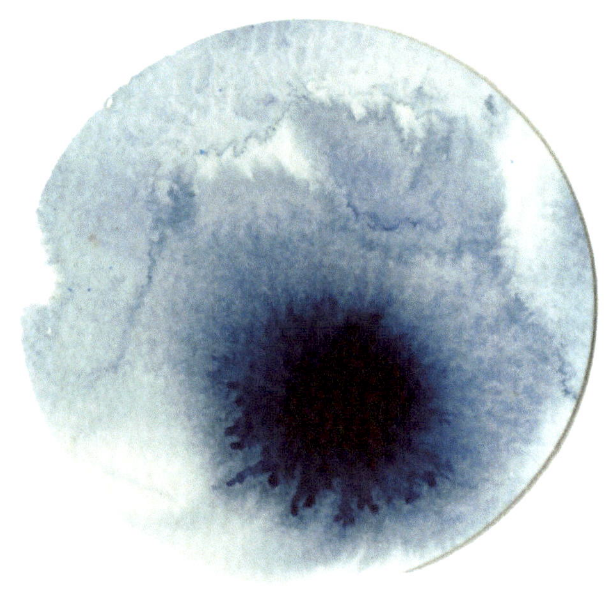

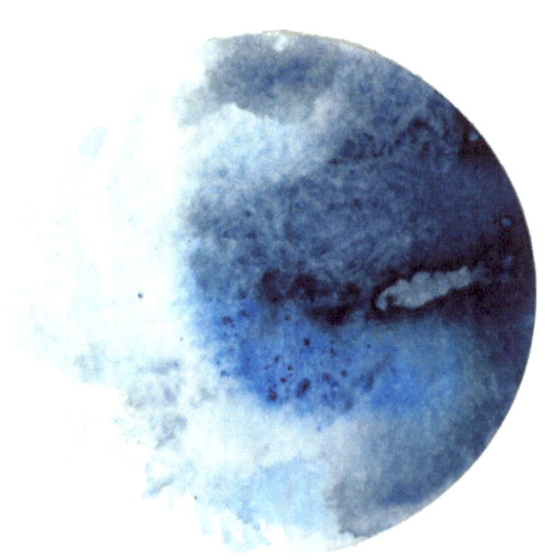

River Risks

When he takes your hand,
you cannot turn back the river
that risked its flow
with force from the mountain's top,

Streams that had all but evaporated
liberate from their springs
roam again the edges where skin touches skin
eyes look beyond eyes.

Heat dissolves through porous parts
Icarus flies upward
does not get consumed,
touching wing tips to
light the sun
brighter.

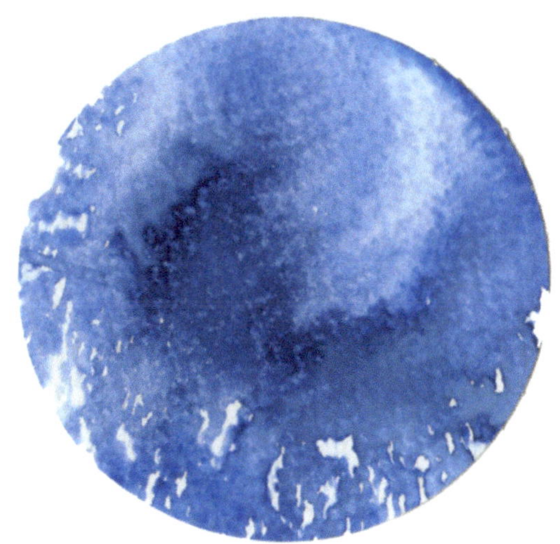

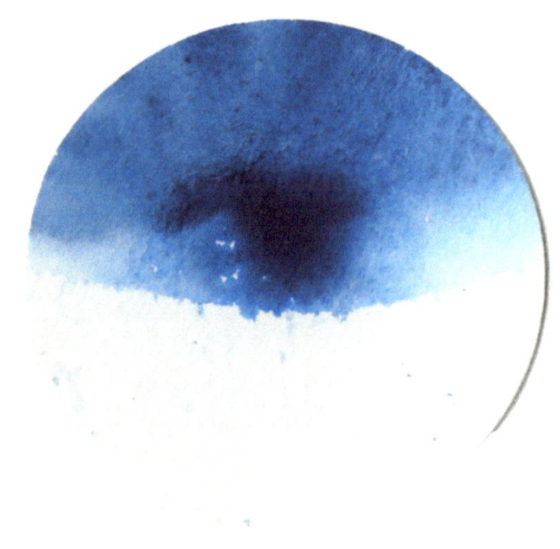

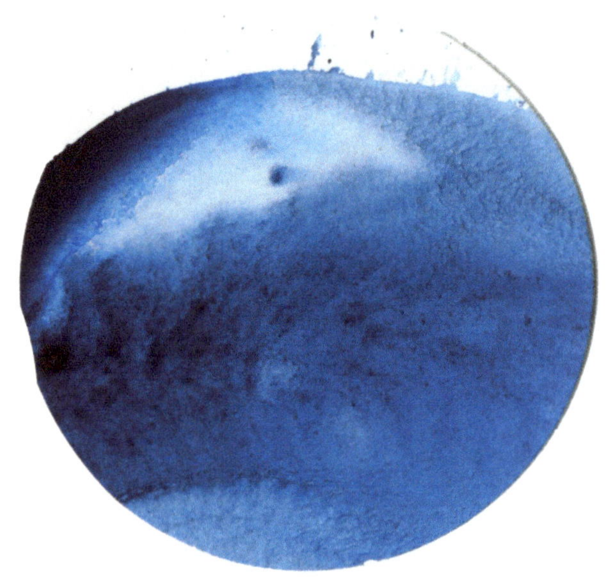

Poems That Wait

Are they waiting for me in the fishbowl?
Goldfish quiver their tails in a C minor key.
Are they waiting in the mountains, along the rough scaly skins of boulders,
barnacles of green yellow lichen that tell the time of sages.

Are they waiting for me under the ice, melting?
Or the Central Park skating rink, where we went as kids,
holding our mittened hands along the length of a woolly scarf.
The end one, often me, sails along
scared to skate so fast, scared to let go and fly.

Poems wait along the window ledge,
keeping me warm inside this changing city,
where I grew up, where I still live.
A city of action, reaction, now restrictive to breathe its air.

Where do poems wait?
In the fridge with ripe cheese and withering apple?
Between the pages of these books on shelves,
in the gaps between their lines?

Tails draw a path where we've been, some known, some imagined.
We lost tails when we shed our fins so long ago,
now hands hold pens,
tap keyboards writing tales of where we are, where we may go,

Is this where the poem waits,
in the space between fingertip and keypad,
between tail and hand, past and present?

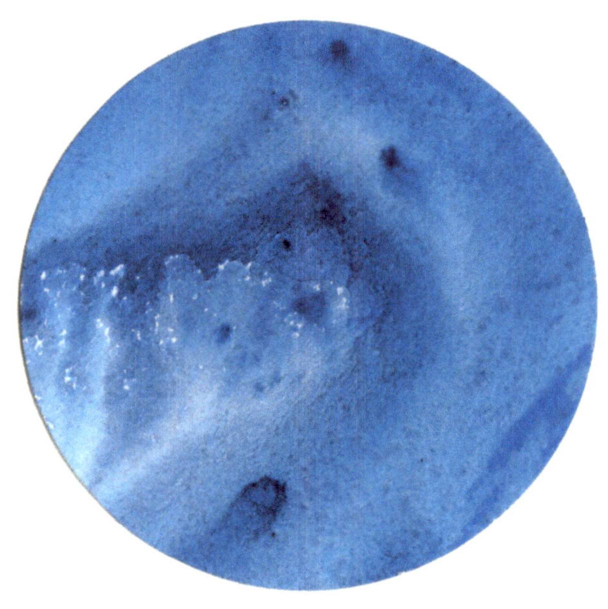

Dear Blur

One is supposed to say 'I miss you' in a postcard, but I am not
sure I do. Blur, you were my first love, my intimate, the one to
see the world through.

You were the face of people gazing at me in stroller, smiling so
I'm told. You were where letters and numbers might have been.
You placed yourself between me and others, we were constant
companions.

Odd to not be in your embrace as I go to bed, and when I wake
to a room that is clear and sharp. Be my ground, my soft edges
my meandering mind that went where it wanted because you
held no harsh borders. Shapes blended as you stood guard.
While I might feel a hard edge here or there as my shin bumped
on a table edge, this didn't harden my images.

Dear Blur, thank you for accompanying me all this time. you live
within me, within each image of my past. And you live between
the sight of many and worlds beyond our eyes.

Book of Times

The book unravels itself
one vein at a time
its spine crumbles
under the weight of indecency
disheveled pages
shed their order
scattering text along the street.

A book for our torn times
all I can do is tear at the paper
then sew it back together
in desire and anticipation.

A book of repulsion
cannot be closed,
its pages of steel repel each other,
their magnetic fields reversed.
Try to close the chapter
you cannot.

A spool of thread
entertains entanglement
to lace the pages red
one thread at a time
a book unstitches itself.

Rolling into itself
this book a circle,
the sun its spine
glows one round page
to the next.

Open the glass pages slowly lest the
upside down miniature
lose the lens' focus
in this book of light.

I think to make a burn book,
whose pages have intimately touched fire
but I cannot.
Burned books are in my blood
and the blood of my people.

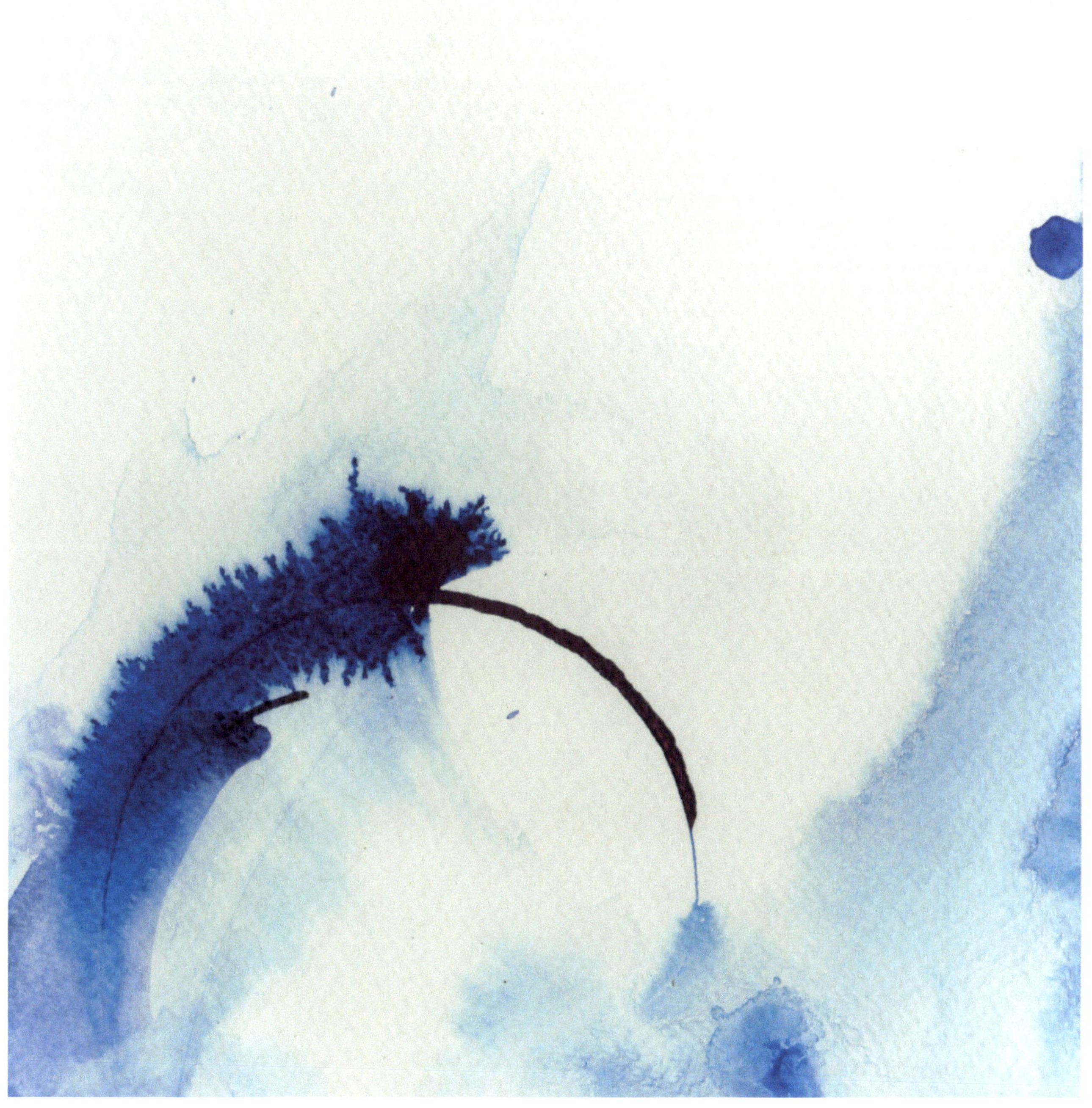

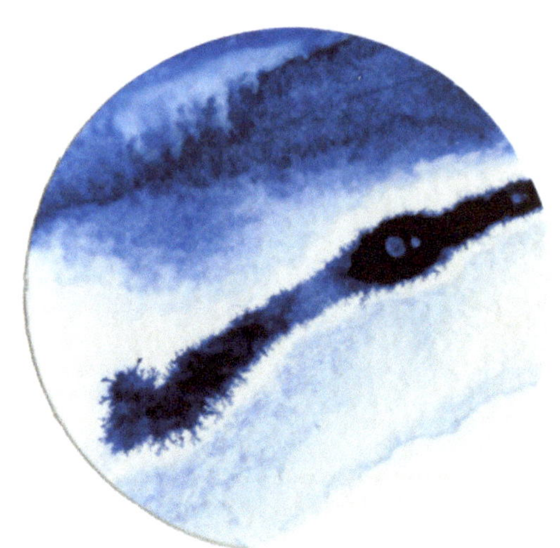

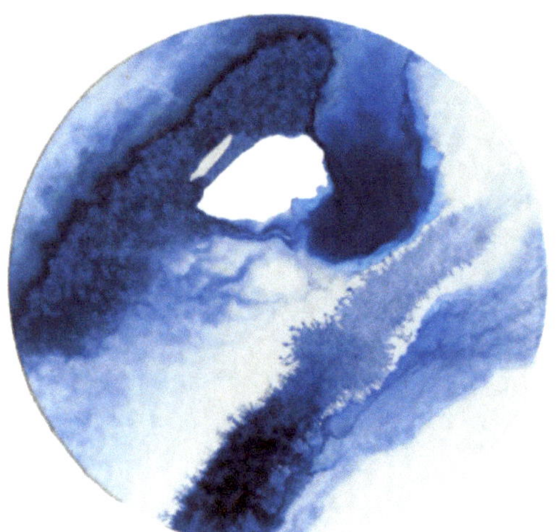

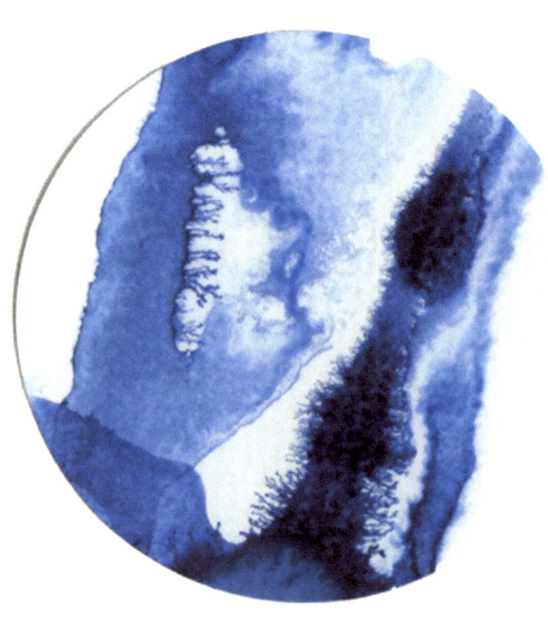

Blue blew blow

I am the dark bowl
I am the pool of water absorbing your marks and masks
your strategies, your breath.

Taste the rain, tie my boots
stop racing for a moment.
Cracks in the old temple wall thick with paper,
centuries of prayer in clefts of time.

Stuffing lists of lists
into openings
this openness
as if I would be blown away
in windy gaps of time.

Indigo spills

Wild as ink let loose
spreads to watery edges
eager as gravity
in the space of a splash

water and inks
continue their dance
unfurling from
each other's mouths

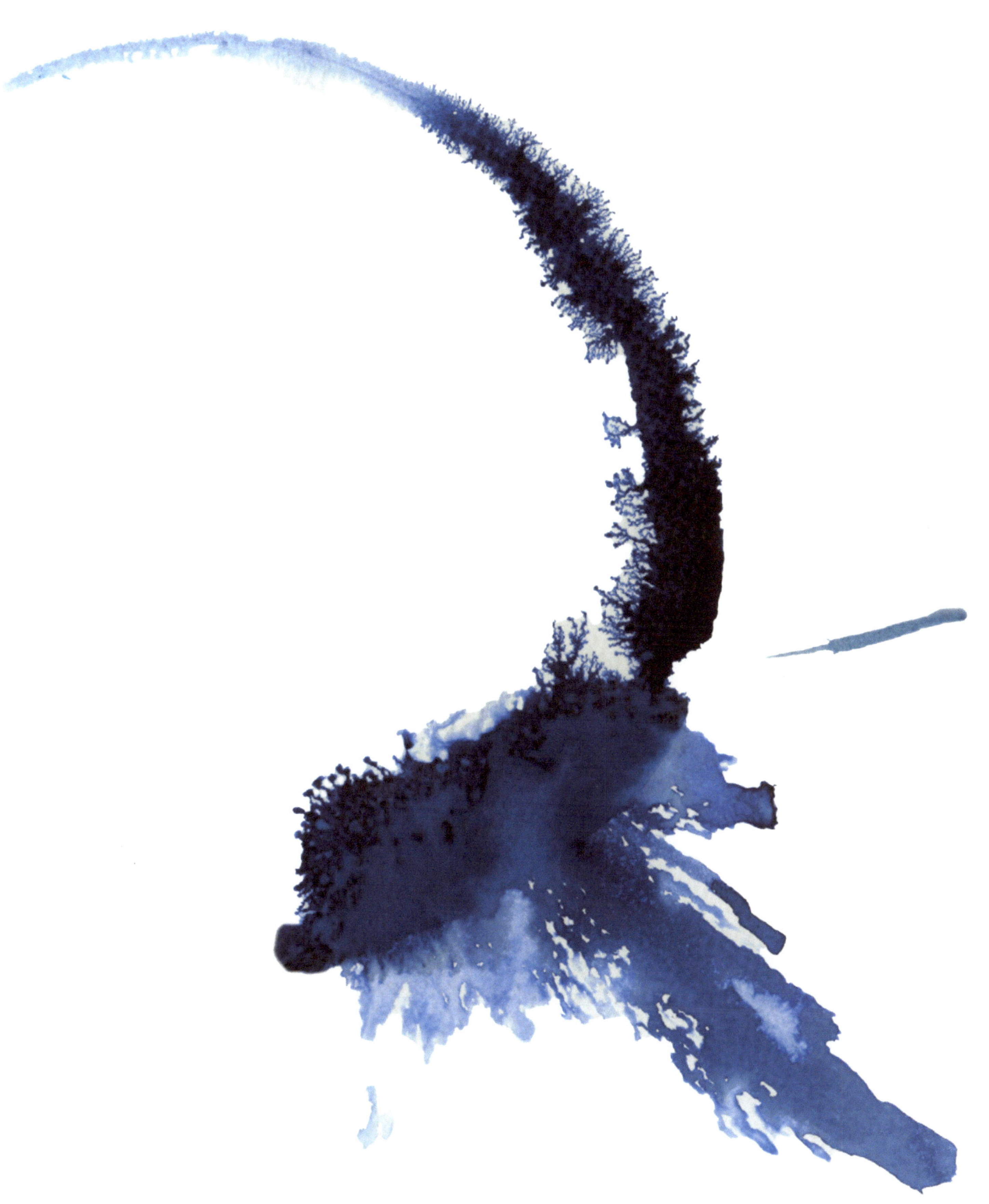

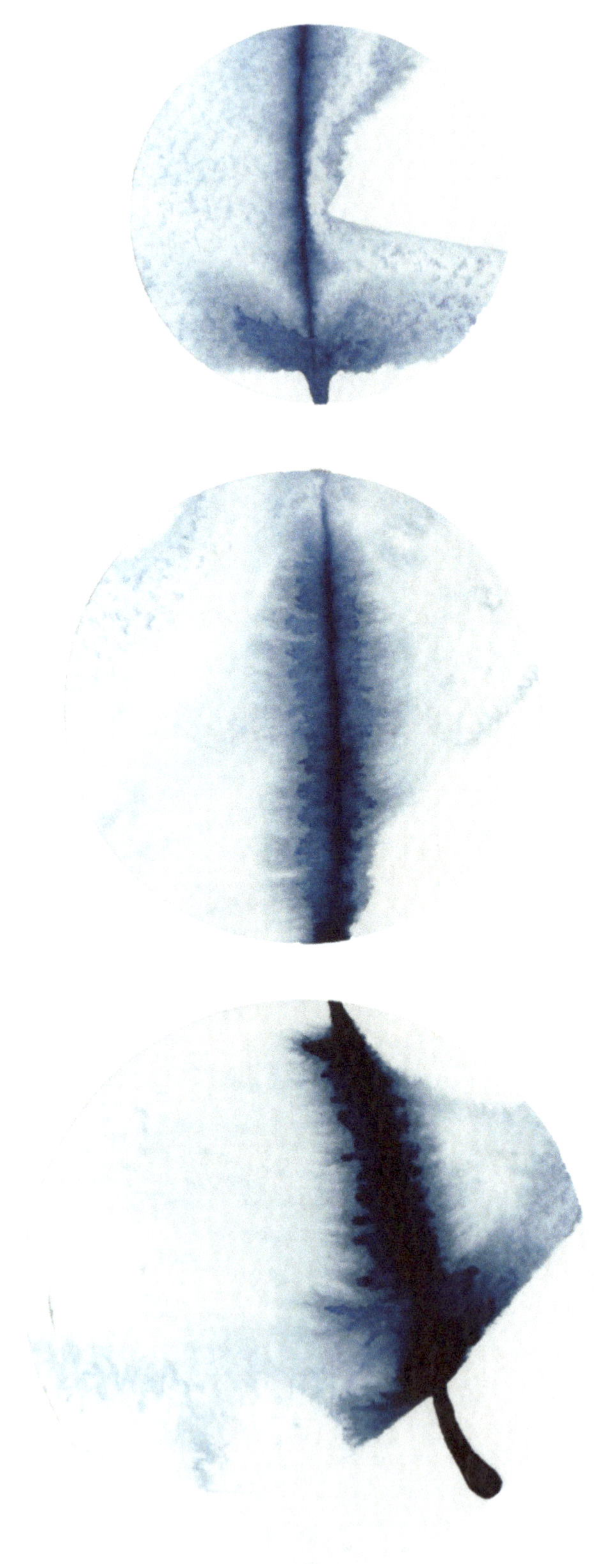

Hide and Seek

Opening my throat
a gulp of indigo travels its width
down my spine, turning veins a deeper shade,
running along an arm's length to
edge my hands.

Hold palms in the air
for the blue to take form,
there is only the space between:
full, palpable and empty.

Ink and words wait formless,
hover midair between damp palms for
somewhere to place themselves.

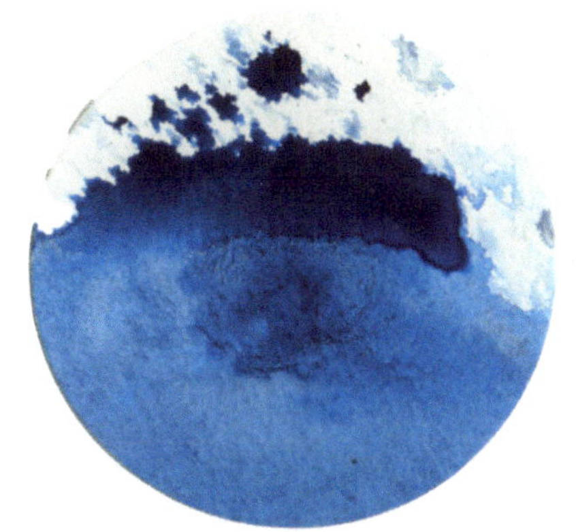

Dust Route

Imagine dust from a pencil as it touches paper,
the sharp point eager
sheds grey powder a little at first
then in an arcing flow, unravels

a silky route through an oasis of graphite
travels for centuries
offerings of sweet and pungent spiced verse
letter and point, line and phrase,
arabesques along
this route of dust.

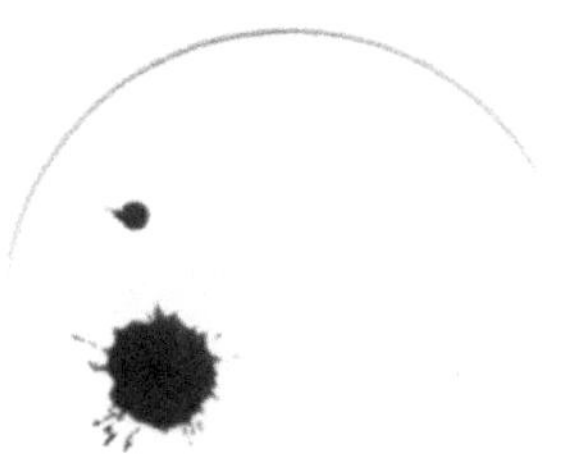

Drawing

I am doing again what I loved as a child
when I learned to see

when I learned to know the world
one object at a time
held close to my myopic eyes,
edges touched with a pencil's tip
marking paper.

This is how I learned to see,
to know form outside my own and
to be seen.

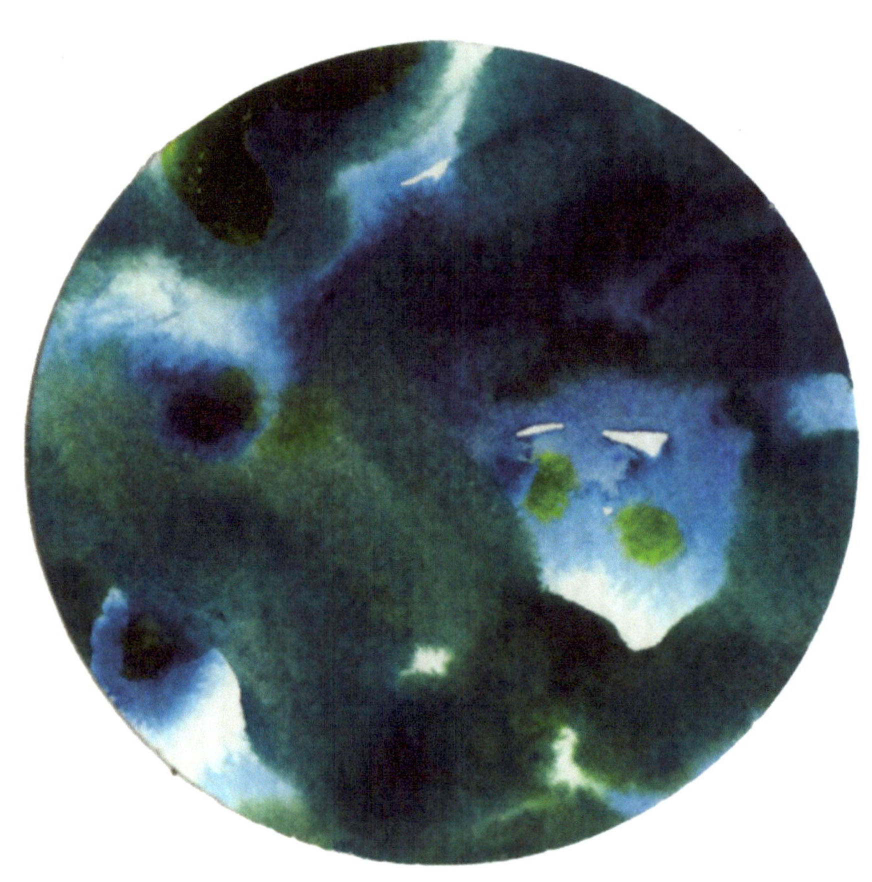

Sea Turtle

In the palm of my hand, at the bottom of a lifeline, a small pool extends to rivers whose flow I do not know. I swim their long branches outward, diving into pale waters that extend from each finger. This is where I meet her.

Is it possible to fall in love with a turtle, to be touched by the space between its shell and mine?

She is a shadow below my fins. Oblong in the center, extensions from all sides. Her form muted against a sandy bottom begins its ascension toward the water's silvery underbelly. I hover, breathing anticipation. Form comes into focus as she leaves the blur of shadows below. Symmetrical patterns map oceans across her flippers and head. Bright yellow and lime green illuminate her sandy sage shell. Floating almost motionless until her fins begin to wave, propelling her slowly upward and foreword. In awe, I mimic this flow, moving my arms in slow circular motion. I too am propelled upward and forward. Above and slightly behind, I let her lead, following her out to sea.

We are swimming in sync. She rises to the surface before me, we poke our heads out breathing air, then dive down into deeper blue green. The gold on her body mirrors the sparkling formations of light rippled on this slice of sea. Gold spills down her head making trenches in the sand that fan out in labyrinthian formation. Ribbons of light extend from this ancient being.

The next morning, in the vast surround of the palest of seas, I swim head above water, my arms making circular patterns, legs kicking rhythmically. I feel her shadow below me though she is not there. The ghost of her voice echoes through water and skin. Her voice is celadon, its tone calm, stable, ancient.

'We are taken care of,' she calls as we swim.

Suzy Sureck is an internationally recognized multidisciplinary artist whose drawings, sculpture and video installations engage physical and metaphoric qualities of natural elements and the poetics of shadow and light. Crosspollinating mediums, her works reach audiences experientially through audio, video, text, and image.

Suzy's works have been exhibited in galleries, museums, sculpture parks, biennials, art foundations and alternative spaces in the U.S., Europe, the Middle East, Korea, Australia, and India. She has been awarded residencies at MassMOCA, Yaddo, Virginia Center for Creative Arts, Art Omi and Arts, Letters Numbers. Suzy received a Masters' Degree in Sculpture from Cranbrook Academy in Michigan and a BFA from the Cooper Union, as well as studies at The Slade School of Art in London. She lives and works in New York City and the Hudson Valley.

For more information, please visit www.suzysureck.com

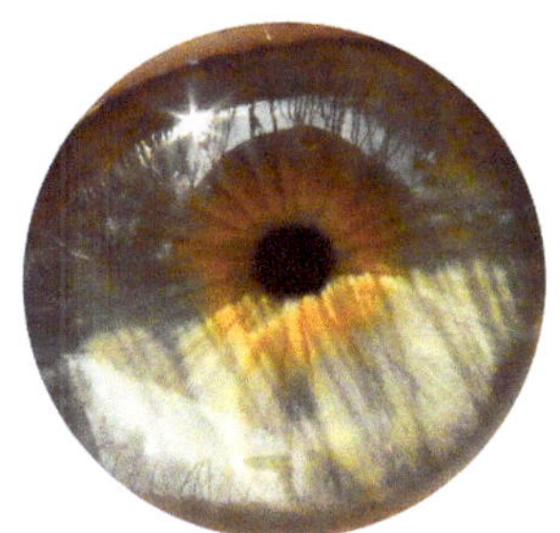